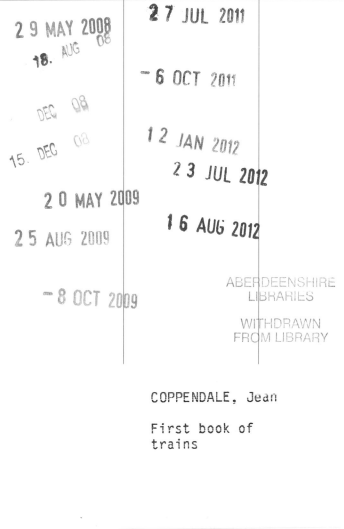

First Book of
TRAINS

Jean Coppendale

QED Publishing

First published in the UK in 2007 by
QED Publishing
A Quarto Group company
226 City Road
London EC1V 2TT

www.qed-publishing.co.uk

A Catalogue record for this book is available from the British Library.

ISBN 978 1 84538 642 9

Written by Jean Coppendale
Designed by Chhaya Sajwan (Q2A Media)
Editor Katie Bainbridge
Picture Researcher Lalit Dalal (Q2A Media)

Publisher Steve Evans
Creative Director Zeta Davies
Senior Editor Hannah Ray

Printed and bound in China

Picture credits
Key: t = top, b = bottom, c = centre,
l = left, r = right, FC = front cover
Joe Osciak: with thanks for image on page 4-5
SBB AG, Bern - Fotodienst/Alain D. Boillat: 5
Jtb Photo Communications Inc/Photolibrary: 6-7, 19
The Glacier Express: 7 t: **Louie Schoeman:** 8-9
CORBIS: Paul A. Souders 9 t
Dave Toussaint Photography: 10-11, 20-21
Paul Lantz: 11 b: **ALSTOM Transport:** 12-13
Denis Baldwin: 14-15
Alamy: Gunter Marx 16-17, Peter Titmuss 17 t
Photo by Fred Guenther: 18-19
Getty: Bruce Hands FC

Words in **bold** can be found
in the glossary on page 23.

Contents

What is a train?

Trains are used to carry people from one place to another. They also carry **goods**, such as cars and coal. A train moves along on tracks.

Some trains carry **passengers** from one city to another.

At the front of
the train is the
driver's cab.
This is where the
driver sits and
makes the train
start and stop.

Train travel

Trains can travel anywhere as long as there is a track. Trains can climb mountains and speed across deserts. They can go over water on bridges and under water in **tunnels**.

Trains sometimes travel through beautiful countryside.

In Switzerland, trains travel through mountains that are covered in snow.

In some places, trains travel through tunnels that are cut into the mountains. They do this if the mountains are too high or too steep to climb.

Steam trains

The first trains used **steam** to make them move along. Huge **furnaces** filled with roaring fires heated water to make steam. The steam worked the engine, which powered the train.

Some steam trains are still in use today. This steam train takes **tourists** along the coast of Namibia, in Africa.

The furnace was at the front of the train. The workers had to shovel coal into the furnace throughout the journey, or the train would stop.

Keeping the fires burning was hot and dirty work. The workers had to be fit and strong.

Freight trains

Freight or cargo trains are used to carry different loads from one place to another. It is cheaper and quicker to transport big, heavy loads by train rather than by road.

A train with lots of wagons can carry huge loads across the country. The wagons can also make the train very long!

All sorts of goods, such as vegetables, furniture and bricks, are carried by freight trains. Freight trains usually travel a long way across the country.

This freight train is carrying new cars to the car sales shop.

Everyday trains

Some trains take people to work in the morning and bring them home again in the evening. These are called **commuter trains**. Commuter trains can get very crowded during the **rush hour**, and people sometimes have to stand.

Many big cities have underground trains which take people to work and school. These trains run every few minutes.

Skytrains

Some trains travel high above the ground. They are called skytrains. These trains move on tracks that are built like a bridge. Skytrains are useful in busy places where there are lots of people.

Many airports and **amusement parks** have skytrains. They can move people a short distance very quickly.

This skytrain is in Detroit, USA. It is controlled by a computer so it does not have a driver.

This skytrain is called a Maglev. It does not have wheels. Instead, it moves along by using **magnets**.

Water no problem!

Trains are very heavy, so a bridge carrying a train has to be very strong.

Big bridges are built over lakes and rivers so that trains can travel across the water. Some bridges have a road as well as train tracks. Cars and trains can cross these bridges at the same time.

Some trains travel under the water. They go through special tunnels.

The Channel Tunnel is a long tunnel that stretches from England to France under the sea. Cars can drive straight onto a special train which takes them through the tunnel.

Express trains

Some trains carry passengers long distances very quickly. These are called express trains. They stop at only a few stations and travel very fast.

This tilting train in the US travels at a very fast speed.

Some express trains can **tilt** over slightly as they go around **curves** in the track. This is so they do not have to slow down.

Some trains have huge windows and a glass roof so passengers can enjoy the view.

Sleeper trains

Some passengers have to travel long distances through the night. Sleeper trains have **carriages** with special cabins. These are where people can sleep and then shower in the morning.

There is also a restaurant on board where passengers can have their meals.

20

Some train journeys can last for many days, so a comfortable bed is important.

Activities

- Collect train pictures from magazines and comics. Put them in a book or on the wall in groups, such as trains that carry people, steam trains, trains crossing a bridge and so on.

- Look at this train. Do you think this is a steam train? Why?

- Make up a story about a train. What kind of train is it? Where is it going? What is it carrying? What happens on the journey?

- Have you been on a train recently? Where were you going? Who were you with? Did you enjoy it? Was the train fast or slow? Full or empty? Draw a picture of yourself on the train.

- Look at these three pictures. Which picture is of train tracks?

  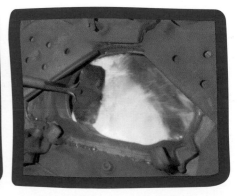

Glossary

Amusement parks
Open-air places with exciting rides, roller coasters and stalls.

Cargo
Items carried in a train from one place to another. Also called freight.

Carriages
The parts of a train where the passengers sit.

Commuter trains
Trains used by people to travel to and from their place of work.

Curves
Lines that bend.

Freight
Items that are carried from one place to another by a train. Also called cargo.

Furnaces
The places where a fire is kept to make steam for the train.

Goods
Things that are bought and sold.

Loads
A large amount of items carried from one place to another.

Magnets
Magnets have an invisible force that pulls things made of steel or iron towards them, or pushes them away. This force is called magnetism. Magnetism moves Maglev trains along the track.

Passengers
People who pay to travel on trains.

Rush hour
Times at the beginning and the end of the working day when large numbers of people travel to and from work.

Steam
Clouds of gas that come from boiling water.

Tilt
When something leans to one side.

Tourist
Someone who travels for pleasure on holiday and goes sightseeing.

Tunnels
Underground passageways for trains.

Index